"In this first book of poems, Hayes Davis bravely reveals love, fatherhood, and loss, truths that stand both on and off the page. As each moment renders its dappled wisdom, the reader suddenly understands: We need such truth —such vulnerability— in the word."

Honorée Fanonne Jeffers

"The long-awaited debut of Hayes Davis is here at last, a complex pattern of experience that builds, poem by poem, into a network of insights binding many identities: son, grandson, life-partner, father, teacher, and most of all, poet. Poems that dramatize the contingencies of family; of its direct influence on the kinds of language we speak, and think and feel with; poems that draw honestly the flight of eros from the domestic scene, as well as the endurance of love & devotion; of small losses that ring through time with rich tones; of secret alienations and internal distances—such poems by Hayes Davis are stirring in their common but difficult recognitions and sensitive portrayals. Even more impressive is how they refract a brilliant, bold set of poems that adopt the mask of Mark Twain's runaway slave, Jim, one of the great characters of American literature. I've often felt, reading Twain's novel, that Jim's nobility and humanity somehow deserve a better narrative, one even more sensitive to the problems of race, difference, and subjectivity. I never expected to find such complementary revisions in contemporary poetry. But it's here that Davis' bold interpolations of Jim's consciousness and interior song, his way of being—his sympathy, fear, regret, sorrow, his morality and heroic love—are recaptured in the texture of his expressive rough nuanced vernacular: these poems by Davis are stunning displays of craft and conscience. They stand out and announce the presence of a new poet we'll want to hear more from soon."

Joshua Weiner

Let Our Eyes Linger

Poems by Hayes Davis

Poetry
Mutual
Press

Poetry Mutual Press

www.poetrymutual.org

ISBN   978-1-365-00519-0

Published 2016 by Poetry Mutual Press.
Printed in the United States of America.

On the cover "Faces" by Earl E. Davis, Jr., photographed by Mignonette Dooley. From the author's private collection.

ACKNOWLEDGMENTS

Grateful thanks to the editors of the publications where some of the poems in this collection first appeared, sometimes in slightly diffferent forms: *Beltway Quarterly, Delaware Poetry Review, Gargoyle, Kinfolks Quarterly, New England Review, Poet Lore.*

"Ali, Bomaye" appears in *Bum Rush the Page: A Def Poetry Anthology*, edited by Tony Medina and Louis Reyes Rivera and published by Broadway Books.

"Carapace" appears in *Gathering Ground: A Reader Celebrating Cave Canem's First Decade*, edited by Toi Derricotte, Cornelius Eady, and Camille Dungy and published by University of Michigan Press.

"Shine" appears in *Full Moon on K Street*, edited by Kim Roberts and published by Plan B Press.

CONTENTS

ONE

TWO

THREE

FOUR

for Teri

ONE

Two Years Later

At 7am Saturday, late autumn easing
through open windows, the bustle
of her son's restless limbs lifts her lids,

settles her barely conscious gaze
on the boy, his eyes, the eyes of the man
who left. A six-year-old knows no weekend.

Saturday means drop-off, the ripped
scab of face-to-face, festering resentments:
the slept-with, best-friend neighbor, the son's

innocent reports of beach trips, skinny dipping
with Anne, Janine. Her bed holds only
this boy, whose stutter has worsened, his throat

clenched with unanswerable questions.
She rises only by compulsion, barely distracts
herself with breakfast and this month's bills

while Sesame Street, Looney Tunes quiet the boy.
When she packs his bag for the week
she imagines his exclamation, how

"Daddy!" always sounds more excited than his return.
She imagines the gnarled, forced small-talk,
imagines looking past the father's face to the paintings

he took when he left—her walls whisper absence,
large spaces outlined in dust—imagines
someone else posing for him, sitting still for far longer

than the drive from Germantown to Roxborough.
In the time it takes to circle the car, unlock
her son's door she decides she can't look

at him, can't force a smile, can't manage
whatever words she'd waste before restarting
the empty car for the drive back to an empty house.

The exterior door reflects her grimace,
the bounce in the boy's step that deflates
when she stops, holds it open, "Go ahead,

I'll see you Friday night." This time he doesn't
stutter: *Aren't you gonna*—"I'll see you Friday."
He runs the thirty feet to his father's door,

knocks, looks back, but she doesn't see
the boy's shoulders slump, doesn't hear him stammer
a reply to *Where's your mother?* doesn't hear

the exasperated exhale, or *I'll be right back.*
Her legs escape just fast enough, his shout swallowed
by just enough distance, the slam of the car door.

Etiquette

I am eight, sitting at my grandmother's
kitchen table, trying to ask to be excused.
My cousins Jennifer and Danielle watch

my open mouth, keep sounding out
"Can...I...be excused" like I don't understand
what I'm supposed to say. They don't know

that "can" is a word I sometimes can't say,
like "hello" when I answer the phone, "goodnight"
when my dad leaves my room, my name

when people ask it. They don't know
that when my teachers' eyes search the class
for an answer, even if I know it I look down.

They don't know that my consonants fly away
sometimes, like birds when it gets too cold.
I stare back at Danielle's mouth, Jennifer's mouth,

Oma's mouth, trying to figure out what makes
talking so easy for them. Maybe my stutter
will go away when I get older.

People on the bus, at the supermarket,
in the candy store always tell me about their
cousins and sisters and brothers, older than me,

who once stuttered like me. They've out-grown theirs,
and I hope mine will disappear one day too, so I won't
miss so many cartoons after lunch.

Perspective

My father praises my stick figures
before sketching the drawing better
than I had. His pencil caresses the paper,
soft shuffle of shading, vanishing point.
His magic populates the sheet—
nebulous contours become people.

Years later, I realize the importance
of his compliment when I walk
my classroom, praise imprecise,
roughly-formed ideas before paraphrasing
in chalk, validating on slate what struggles
forth after late nights of reading.

When their sketches rival the drawings
I've planned after reading, annotating a text
a little like his long hours at an easel
I feel almost as proud as I imagine my father
when I brought home the drawing he matted,
framed, hung near his own exquisite creations.

Route 1 North, Philadelphia to Highland Park

Your father has given you the wheel.
The mostly-empty highway offers
your 17 year-old road eyes no distractions,
and the Firebird descending the on-ramp is red.

The left turn signal isn't instinctive yet.
Nor is the glance that checks your blind spot
before the lane change. But as you settle
back into the forward focus of highway driving

your father's hand covers your gearshift-perched
right, his mouth curling before opening, "Good job."
He doesn't remind you that sharing the road
with newcomers is less instinctual for you

than your blind-spot check. He is all praise,
and when the therapist asks, ten years later,
what you miss—how you imagined him
feeling when you pictured handing over

the grandchild he will never know—you remember
that he never held praise too tightly, that he
knew confidence as a vested commodity,
its installation as vital as anything fathers give sons.

Fridays at Acme

My grandmother pauses in the door of the market, remembering
what she's there for. People excuse their way past. She frowns

at the small, pale tomatoes, remembers Summer Jersey Reds
she used to buy on the way to and from Mantaloking.

The deli selection wasn't so vast when she was growing up.
The clerk asks *Can I help you?* Oma is still deciding, but says

"What?" anyway and the clerk repeats his question.
In front of the juices she looks over all the bottles,

all the brands, all the flavors while people repeat *Excuse me,*
wait patiently and smile at me as I gently put my hand on her back,

say *People are trying to get by.* She turns to them, smiles, says
"I'm sorry," in a louder voice, pointing at her hearing aid.

She speaks softly, though, when she tells me what else she needs:
"Parmalaat milk, Maier's I-talian bread and Bayer Baby Aspirin."

Frozen dinners and pot pies have been around a long time;
she easily picks out chicken and turkey while I find the aspirin.

At the checkout, flipping through coupons, she catches me
looking at my watch. "Where you gotta be?"

Nursing Home

Mommy De recognizes my diploma.
Her smile reaches her eyes, she parts her lips,

and mumbles a string of words her mind
has tried to sort into a sentence—she's almost as happy

about my degree as she was when I walked in the room.
I think of the day my mother received her Master's

from Penn, and I'm glad that my grandmother
could speak her joy clearly then. As pleased as I am

that she can spill messy, jubilant recognition
when I come to visit, I feel a little guilty that mom

has to call herself "Bethy," to answer the inevitable
"Who are you," coax a smile of semi-memory.

The fact that Mommy De recalls my face, if not my name
makes me uneasy when I think of my uncle Conrad

who is never "Henry," "brother," or another alias
used to mask the disease, just a man with a beard

who never stays for as long as he has driven to visit.
Even my aunt Annette, who shares that name with her mother,

lives in the same city and visits more often than me
is never someone Mommy De knows on sight.

I put my diploma away, produce graduation pictures
hesitantly, reluctant to identify three children to their mother.

TWO

American Literature

We discuss Harlem Renaissance poetry.
But discuss is the wrong verb,
at least at the beginning of class
when their fourteen silent stares focus
on their desks—they don't look

at each other, and no one looks at me,
not even the one black student in class.
His shoulders seem to slump like mine.
Does he, like me, fight the desire
to leave the room, frustrated by the unspoken...

What is it? Guilt? Defiance? Belief
that these carpeted hallways insulate us
from the clamor of McKay's cultured hell?
Do they believe Obama's election
has burned off the fog of oppression,
rendered irrelevant the laments of the past?
Do they fear a word dropped careless
in the room? Did they learn silence
from parents more scared of race than puberty?

When one hand breaks the stillness, I tiptoe
with language, dance through scansion,
poetic devices, try to allay their fear
of screaming indictment, stern reminder:
what some of their ancestors did to some of mine.

The conversation moves cautiously
to the ending couplet. Later,
the black student reads "I Too Sing America"
and I know he hears himself in the poem.

I catch his eye as he walks slowly
toward the door and our gaze
says far more than we could if we spoke.

Black Boy, Independent School

Early June, summer camp, three months
before Pre-K, "How'd he do?" tossed to the teacher
like a beach ball. But she cocks her head,

"Well..." raises her hands, wiggles her fingers,
and suddenly the foreboding swirl of class and race
that sat on your shoulder as you watched your daughter

wade the early waters of private school augurs
your son's entry. He listened quietly as you counseled her
to use words, not hands, so you wait to hear

"he wasn't the only one." You wait for reports
of provocation but get only that he also threw toys.
You promise conversation, "Perhaps it's just transition"

and the next day is worse, and the next, and the next
and now the language reminds you of staffings
at the private school where you teach—black boys

who distract the class, validated by laughter, black boys
who thrive in the hallway and vanish in the classroom
behind lowered expectations, or mid-season exhaustion,

hour and a half-long commutes. Perspective vanishes
behind every story you've watched up close and afar,
behind every "he's so bright" and "so much potential"

behind pained hallway testimonials. You hope he won't
swallow punchlines, smile through slights, accept
their projections. You hope he will hear no unspoken

question in their gaze. So many independent schools
chew so many black boys, spit some defeated, some self-loathing,
some passed through, some used up, two what-could-have-beens

for every confident stride across the stage. And yet you
and your wife chose this path for him, this boy who asked
at three "Mommy, do we have to stay on the road?" You want

to feed his brain, open doors and windows but you hope
he keeps his legs, you hope that you, his father, long versed
in the subtle languages of these spaces, can translate for him,

help him pick his way along this path. You hope you can
pick him up, refill the confidence unconscious bias saps.
Maybe summer will settle his spirit, maybe it really is just transition,

maybe black boys can just be boys, but "maybe" does not massage
your shoulders when your phone lights up with a call
from his classroom in the first week of the new school year.

Capitol Hill, SE

I might have called it an experiment,
but I had no hypothesis when I dressed

in sneakers, baggy jeans, Iverson jersey, parka,
dangled a half-smoked Black & Mild from my mouth,

not unlike a James Dean cigarette. Most white
faces glanced cautiously at my swagger, chose

to offer no greeting as we passed. The averted eyes,
clenched mouths usually exchanged pleasantries

with my khakis, sweater, top coat. My study
clarified when I encountered black and brown people

dressed in suits—they maintained eye contact, spoke
even while a few kept a safe distance. A warmth

in their eyes said *we see you,* and I realized I was watching
myself trying not to ignore young, hard-looking brothers

even while feeling a little anxious on the nights
when I'm the one dressed in khakis, a sweater, a top coat.

Nigger Apple

The sticker on the watermelon said "seeded."
I grimaced, imagining hundreds of small eyes
staring at me even as I spit them out,
DuBois' dual consciousness come to culinary life.

Did the cashier share my vision?—she wrapped
bag after bag around the complicated, heavy orb.
I stopped her after four, content quick glances
wouldn't see through the layers, might think
"Magruders," not "Just like it says in the encyclopedia!"

Walking out of the store I thought of the student
who read DuBois in my class and confessed
that even before he put a name to his second set of eyes
he never ate fried chicken in the student lounge.

I wondered when it started, when the sphere grew large
and inconvenient, when I began to see myself
and myself as through a glass darkly—perhaps
after my mother took offense at the pastor

who said through a smile he "just knew" I loved basketball,
or the fiftieth McDonald's chicken ad populated
only by black faces. Maybe the watermelon grew
heavy with my help, nurtured by an identity too dual,
more conscious of history than taste.

At home, blinds drawn, I licked my lips,
sliced through the striped shell. I pictured
1930s cartoons, grinning mouths separating
bite after bite of red from rind—
but the red I exposed was too dark,
the insides over-ripe, sweetness soured, spoiled.

Inundated

What tides move in him? At what watermark
did survival instinct kick in? How much water
is too high for wading? At what pitch
of a baby's cry does the father think *diapers*,
food, instead of *too deep, too much wind?* On film

his trudge out of the French Quarter Walgreens
will be labeled "LOOTING," his visage, gait
indistinguishable (to the casual viewer)
from people clutching stereos, sneakers, alcohol,
any item the newsroom seems to suggest
black people grab first. But look closely:

see Huggies under his right arm, gallon of milk
gripped in his left hand. Who can know his story?
Who wouldn't grab a 12-pack, if the bad day
that sends you to Scotch on a Tuesday
were strung together for months, for lifetimes,
if what a teenager makes working a summer job
had to feed a family, if healthcare, a house
were fleeting dreams? So look again—

he carries milk with the Huggies and he's
black and he might not have made it home but you
wouldn't, probably, have heard if he didn't so call him
father, or husband, maybe Larry, or Junior, handsome,
thoughtful, drenched, scared, but not "Looter."

Shine

The last night in February is warm.
Light rain clouds around street lamps,
creates rainbow mists that color avenues
different shades of empty Sunday night.

The ROOTS' new CD reaches from the speakers,
distracts our ears from the squeak
of the pothole-weary front axle with crisp taps
on the side of the snare, brisk walks on the high hat

laced under Black Thought's verbal jabs.
We drive slowly past brothers on corners. One raps
the last verse of "Double Trouble." His voice possesses
a peace that matches the night. His smile mirrors

his friends', so different from scowls affected
on the covers of *Vibe*, *Blaze*, *The Source*.
At Lincoln and North Capitol several black men,
young and old, discuss the fallacy of a released

but voteless felon and the displacement inherent in
urban development. I won't tell you how refreshing
it is to hear what I heard—but later I sleep
more quietly, waking only to look at the street lights.

"Ali, Bomaye"

Right hand lead
pure disrespect sends
Foreman into frenzy
fists swinging anger
like a son trying to chop
huge father-lynching tree down.

Ali raises fists on ropes,
blocks punch after punch
trades jab after jab
seven rounds, Foreman tires,
Ali pounces from the corner
swinging "boom! boom!"

George Foreman falls.

Ali circles, watches
wounded victim struggle,
artist contemplating
the canvas "Big George"
is crumpling to—he
is one more victim
fulfilled prophecy
of Muhammed.

Then monsoons pour
stadium onto roads
jumping chanting
strong in early morning,
Ali riding past
Zaire, past faces

shining in rain, Ali
watching Zaire
standing, so tall.

Ivory

Start at his hand, not grasping
though this trunk is precious with promise.

Follow the gentle curve to his brother's—
this much potential is so heavy their hands

heft together, balance the burden, the possibility
of this ivory polished, sundered into earrings,

necklaces, gentle carvings of small elephants.
Follow from their hands to the

end of the tusk where the body begins,
another tusk promising more prosperity,

waiting to be freed from the perfect stillness,
the liberator frozen mid-swing, his body

all business, ligament and muscle mid-flex,
the axe poised, anticipating its work

gleaming blade catching the sun and look
at the sky, clouds complementing the ivory,

white patches blotted gently against blue.
Look one more time at the trees' gently

reaching branches, their line picked up
by the brush that leads your eye back

to the brothers, gazes fixed on the tusk,
calculations grazing in their heads.

Tactile

The father does not hug his son long enough.
The son carries his suitcase upstairs, unpacks
neatly, hangs shirts, pants, jacket, belt.

Return, routine eases the gut-punch of grief,
but he washes his face quicker than before,
turns off the bathroom light, tries not to see

his grandmother accidentally trapped in her basement,
banging on the door as hard as a 91-year-old woman
can before collapsing. He sets the alarm, tries

to imagine shaving and ironing the next morning,
instead of Oma's frenzied calls to Aunt Peggy,
the brass handle's stubborn immobility,

frantic thuds growing louder, quicker, quiet.
He climbs into bed, curls up, cries briefly,
but without tears—in this house grief

is the bust of his dead stepmother sculpted
by the father who never worked in clay, the son's
poems about that stepmother, who asked the Lord

for "two good years" with Earl and died twenty five
months later. Grief comes to this house
through the hands, and this week grief will

debone chickens, slice the collards and red onions.
Grief will iron black ties and white shirts, design
the funeral program, sift photos for the cover.

Table Manners

He sips the wine, remembers Oma's glass-a-day
(red, "doctor's orders"). He stares at the placemats
she gave him for Christmas. He imagines her
prophetic, knowing one month later he would pray
in earnest, thankful for the pattern to remember her by.

He wonders if she meant something by dying,
if she heard his complaints that the family never gathered
anymore, that Aunt Peggy's house used to be filled
with food and spirit. He believes she brought
his estranged half-brother back, and he remembers

Oma's smile on the back of the funeral program,
curled mouth, flashing eyes, so like his father's
description of the taste of cilantro, "a little bit of spring."
But he thinks he shouldn't wonder about prophecies,
assign meaning to her death because he still believes
she died too early at 91. He looks at the flowers

on the placemats, remembers the repast at Aunt Peggy's—
the food line stretched around the dining room, laughter
thicker than mac and cheese, Oma's great-grandchildren
running through the house, the littlest ones' faces
blessed with newness, a little bit of cilantro.

September

In the middle of a sentence of advice, the first wave
takes his legs, salt water conspiring with the diabetes.
For the first time you see your father fall.

Sitting on the wet sand, his legs covered with the surf,
he laughs. It's genuine, not the uneasy, self-deprecating
chuckle he used to relate the story of the day last summer

when he wet his pants. The next wave comes as he's
struggling to stand up, gripping the hand you've extended
and as this wave takes him from your grasp you feel a little

of what it might be like when he slips more finally away.
The wave rolls him towards the beach and he comes to rest
again, this time on all fours and not laughing. His hair

is damp, white with sand. He sputters water from his mouth.
And before he tries to stand again the wave recedes,
taking him with it. You stand in front of him, stopping

him with words you thought were made only to be spoken
back: "I've got you." Then the sea relaxes, lets you help him up.
Part of you feels proud, like you've passed a test. Part of you

wants to fall, let him pick you up once more. Later,
when you watch him stretched sleeping on the blanket, his
confession of feeling "helpless" still echoes uncomfortably.

Carapace

I.

The hand on my father's back is curious
even as it tries to comfort. What is the essence
of these bones that feel like rocks under a tent?
Where will I go with this jagged feeling,
new knowledge of his insides? Can I look

that closely, notice crag and crevice,
or is the feeling too new, too sharp?
What will the stones do in my stomach,
my mouth? What kind of geology is this?
Island Beach used to be our summer comfort—
soon he will rest there, stones to sand to water.

II.

Comfort for now is cool washcloths
on his forehead, Jolly Ranchers
after days of Thorazine sleep,
a nurse just a little gentler than the last.
Comfort will be tubes removed, an ambulance
home, dressing in his clothes,

drinking from his own glasses, wearing
his own underwear. His house filled with people,
the quiet when they leave.

III.
Comfort is helping him pee, or lifting him
onto the toilet, waiting, wiping after his bowels
stir reluctantly. Sitting up with him when he

is afraid to sleep, laughing quietly, writing
the obituary, as if listening to old stories—
his body running cross country, riding a motorcycle—
will smooth stones, slow time.

Vessel

The beach as I had never seen it: November, wind
that wasn't breeze, sun that wasn't warm, surf that held
the odd smile of scattering his ashes in the place he loved.
The sky stretched in cliché. I hugged the urn. We stood

in a circle, a radio played "Hymn to Freedom." I didn't want
to let go, didn't want to let go. My brothers and I
carried him to the water. So many ashes, a pile
on the wet sand. The surf came, swept. We walked

back up the beach. I turned, watched until the surf took
everything— dust, chips, fragments, took my father out to sea.

The Caldor Apocalypse

I believe the world's end
will look something like this:
A nearly empty store, fixtures
dismantled, leftover items thrown

helter-skelter into a scattered mass
of brown plastic shopping carts.
Gleaners sift those vessels
for hidden answers, as if they might

find souls among fragments
of olive green carpet, faded orange
t-shirts, the metallic mauve wrapping paper
no one buys, even at 50 cents a roll.

Children shuffle across the dirty floor,
pointing at undersized baseball gloves,
one armed dolls. Parents answer
with a distracted, automatic "No."

The security guard is amused by his
own presence. Nothing here is worth
the risk of a criminal record.
Some have found an answer or two,

wait in lines longer than purgatory,
gripping cash or a Visa. All sales are final.

Tilling

Listening to Outkast, the modern incarnation
of Funkadelic – "Dad would've liked this." Admiring
his art on our walls, remembering his talent

in a sweet, sad way like an ex-lover. Reading
baseball standings: Philly's in first. Remembering
he liked Dave Brubeck, playing "La Paloma Azul"

again, and again. Watching Scorcese's camerawork,
Morgan Freeman's eyes. The insurance money
was flowers, pleasant shrubs covering the moody soil

with nonchalant purchases, the promise of a house.
It felt so good I walked to the first therapy session
in the early spring night, allergy medicine

suppressing sneezes, congestion. I emerged dirty,
eyes red, the flowers smothered by upturned earth,
pleasant shrubs clipped, scattered. And it's raining—

drops drumming as the mud thickens, spreads.
I long for the next planting season, a new landscape.

Repair

Spring—abundant rain, recovering lawn
strengthened by two fertilizer treatments.
Hedges boast verdure, annuals flourish,
pastel hues nudge away memories

of last summer's drought. My father loved
azaleas, but now when they return, fuschia slicked
with days of steady downpour, I don't linger
in front of his paintings, search for pictures

of him standing. I smile at the color of the bushes,
consider the rich, late-evening light, the backyard
dappled with sun, the scent of ginger-marinated
chicken on the grill. When a thud escapes

the bedroom window, I know the fragile body sculpture
I just re-hung has fallen, but I don't rush inside,
upstairs, fighting tears. I turn the chicken,
ask confirmation through the window screen,

think *Strosniders, wood glue, replacement nails.*
I use his hammer to rebuild the frame, return the piece
to the wall, but it escapes me that it's Father's Day.
Eight years has dulled the sharp edge of empty.

THREE

Angels

Only thing Huckleberry ever say about his Pap
besides how much he drank, cussed
was how bad he beat Huck, chased
him round the room night before Huck left.
Pap so drunk he said snakes was on him,
so drunk he called his son the Angel of Death.

Death supposed to make faces peaceful.
Someone supposed to close our eyes for us.

My Nanna she looked happy—she said she
saw her Betsy waiting for her, said she
saw her Robert waiting for her, said she
couldn't wait to tell them bedtime stories said she
missed that most when they got sold away.

Before the Widow's Mr. Daniel died
he told her not to miss him, told her
he was sorry he never gave her a son.
When his chest stopped moving she
covered him, braced up like she always did,
cried when she thought no one could hear.

But Pap, laying dead in this house
that floated our way after the storm
ain't really smiling, ain't really angry.
Look scared, like whoever shot him gave him
time to think about what was coming.

Jim on the Raft after His "Dream"

The snake in my bed on Jackson's Island
wasn't trick enough—now Huck tell me I
dreamt the fog, his canoe cut loose from the raft,

say I *dreamt* two hours searching for the only
white person who might not turn me in.
He ask if I been drinking, look me

in the eye and say he been here all along.
This got to stop if we gonna make it down river,
make it to Cairo and the free states, but I play along

for now—"looky here, boss, dey's sumf'n wrong!"
I give him one more chance—boy only 14,
far from home, friends, whoever he call family.

I tell him what we both know: the fog, us whooping
trying to find each other, mixed up among the tow-heads
and islands, raft almost grounded, me almost drowning.

But he dig in harder than a rat-chasing pup,
call it a staving dream, ask me tell him about it.
Sunrise pushing night out the sky, birds singing,

he study my face while I "terpret" the dream,
painting everything up as warnings, saying we be okay
if we mind our business, stay off land for now.

While he watching me I'm trying to decide
how much daddy talk he might take from a nigger.
When I finish he ask what the mess on the raft stand for,

and my voice bite sharper than I thought it ever would
around any white person, even a boy. His eyes bug out,
he stare at me, then he set his jaw, walk off, stay

on the far corner of the raft for fifteen minutes.
When he come back slow, mouth quivering, apologizing,
I let my breath out. Later he ask why I

didn't beat a tin pan in the fog, keep beating it
till we found each other. He get real quiet when I
ask how many runaways he know *want* attention.

The "King" and "Duke" Join the Raft

Tried to tell that boy we
doing fine by ourselves,
need to leave well enough alone.

This "Duke" remind me
of Tom Sawyer and his tricks.
This "King" could be Huck

in 30 years. But Petersburg
way back up river and they
ain't sneaking out to play

robbers and bandits, so I
can't even pretend to sleep—
Huck still running from his daddy,

can't see the King look just like Pap,
smell almost as drunk, looking
for even quicker money.

Huck too busy missing Tom
to see the Duke wouldn't mind
making fools out of both of us.

All they see is property
floating on a raft with a boy
who give them half our food.

When they go to town talking
"figure a way to run in the daylight"
Orleans seem closer twice as fast.

When they print a runaway notice
describing me better than Mama could,
I'm glad I sent the boy with them for coffee.

Bound

Back up river at Miss Watson's we had
horn to wake us up, bell to send us to the field.

Sometimes seem like all I hear was
horns and bells, bells and horns.

But now I reckon worrying about Miss Watson
pecking at one of us for walking a little tired

better than laying here day after day tied up
while Huck and them scoundrels trick town

after town out of its money, make sure
their insurance, meaning me, don't run off.

Ropes get tight if I move, belly tighter
when the sun get high.

Every shout in the distance sound like
trouble coming closer. Every snapped twig

sound like catcher footsteps.
Day before yesterday I heard

a runaway getting' chased—
dogs first, five pairs of feet next—

and I trembled and sweated
more than an hour after they voices faded.

Sent Her Sprawling

I choose a night with no moon to tell Huck
about the time I slap 'Lizbeth for not listening.

It's quiet except for tree frogs and crickets
singing to bring some pretty thing closer.

Least that's what Nanna used to say
to get us children not to be scared of the dark.

He listen real close when I mention scarlet fever,
get even quieter when I say she went sprawling.

I figure maybe he remember his daddy's fists so I
tell how I realized she was deaf, started crying.

When I finish the story, he don't ask if I'm sorry—
he ask how far from Miss Watson's my wife live,

how far from there 'Lizbeth and Johnny is,
if I think they still together, how I think

we gonna make it back up river to them. I don't
know how to answer—afraid to hope, afraid not to.

The "Rescue"

Mister and Missus Silas pray with me.
Tom want me to keep a pet rattlesnake.

Mister Silas check on me, share his tobacco.
Tom want me to keep a mullen-stalk, water it with tears.

Missus ask me about my Johnny, l'il 'Lizbeth.
Tom want me to write in my blood.

Missus ask me if I got enough to eat, if I'm comfortable.
Tom throw a piece of my meat to the dogs.

Huck say I don't need a journal or a rope ladder.
Tom say I need them and a coat of arms, need to dig a moat.

He want to send me an onion in my coffee
to make tears to water the mullen-stalk.

He snuck a spoon in my corn pone—I about
mashed out my teeth biting it, but he told me

sharpen the spoon to write in blood on my shirt.
He say scratch marks on a tin plate, throw it out the window.

They take off my chain so I can help Huck
roll a grindstone into my cabin. Tom watch us,

directing, all the time asking Huck if they need to catch
more rats to keep me company, how many spiders Huck

figure it take to make cobwebs for "atmosphere."
I draw the line at the rattlesnake.

Jim Observes a Class

I.
Teacher ask his students
If I really had a family.

He ask his students
If I cared for that boy.

He ask his students
If I lied about 'Lizbeth.

He ask his students
If I even had a daughter to hit.

2.
Sometimes I tell Huck the truth.
Sometimes I tell Huck what he need to hear.

Some nights I stand his watch because he say he tired.
Some nights I don't know how long he can stay awake.

Sometimes we just talk and laugh and talk some more.
Sometimes I know he's worrying about helping a runaway.

Some days I just need him to help me stay free.
Some days I just want to make sure he stay safe.

FOUR

Chinese Take-Out Dream

Turning from our small talk to the man behind the counter
your eyes dart across the board, settle on Szechwan Shrimp
wrapped in tortillas with chestnuts and almonds. As your lips
form "Szechwan" the ambient hum of Saturday night hustle

stops, looks at you, hangs on every word that floats
on pastel blue clouds from your lips to the man's hand holding
the Bic pen that waits to trail ink across the order pad. The pen
almost forgets how to write because it's trying to remember

the last time it saw clouds and words like yours. The hand
holding the pen almost forgets how to move, for the same
reason. The Bic remembers the platinum-plated fountain pen
from the nice part of town, her smooth ink. The hand

remembers the rainy day when its owner got asked out
by a French manicurist. The hand and pen smile, push
across the order sheet. You turn back to me, ask what I'm
doing later, and the sun comes out from behind the jukebox.

Groove

Their feet own a pattern on the dance floor.
Years of love have practiced this improvisation.
Their ears know the inside walls of the bass
and their legs are possessed by the speakers.

Years of love have practiced this improvisation
that makes jealous couples head for the door.
Their legs are possessed by the speakers,
share space that fits in warm grooves of vinyl.

Jealous couples who don't head for the door
marvel at movement of pelvis to legs to funk.
Sharing space that fits in warm grooves of vinyl,
the dancers don't feel anything but the hip shake.

Marvelous movement of pelvis to legs to funk
shows their ears know the inside walls of the bass.
The dancers don't feel anything but the hip shake
their feet own a pattern on the dance floor.

Library

It's almost a cliché—he walks the library, gazing
but not quite lingering these last few days before retirement.
He appreciates the variety: some students sweating
through quadratic equations, others searching allegory,

allusions for meaning, one just reading *Rolling Stone*.
Here's a teacher, organizing the approaching 70 minutes
into stimulus, process, reflection. Here's a girl sleeping,
curled small on a couch, her breathing easy, so different

from the bundle of energy that will emerge later
from 8th period, ready to run, release before settling into
her French workbook. He casts these images, preserves them
along with the smell of books, the soft shuffle of paper,

furious typing that anticipates a deadline—all the sounds and sights
he will remember, but not hear when he leaves this place.

New English Teacher

"Did Mary have the talk with her?"
I ask when Louise tells us the new mother
has taken the job. I know the answer,
but I ask anyway, the question almost

a voice of protest, a warning
from a half-drowned man: this water
will swallow a marriage, the joy of cooking
or reading for pleasure. We can swim

one of those strokes, maybe two, but some
of our delights inevitably sink, lost amid
essays begging attention, pencil marks, guidance,
or quizzes whose jumbled voices struggle

to recall the previous night's reading.
Even when their young minds send us floating
into a weekend with pride, new insight into books
we thought we knew cover to cover, the undertow

always steals our legs, makes a Sunday stroll
through a museum an idle daydream. But maybe
she'll show us how it's done, discover some secret
formula, equal parts home, work, child, leisure.

Or maybe she'll just join us as we
tread water, tread water, tread water.

Redefined

Years ago the paddleboat
would have been a rowboat,
my t-shirt: long-sleeves
and a tie, blazer, straw low-topper.
You assuredly <u>not</u> in jeans, but a
white dress over petticoats, chemise,
corset. Gloves, of course, a jaconet
and parasol to deflect the sun.

It would still be Sunday
but a chaperone might have watched
from the hill, instead of groundhogs.
The Old Lyme, Connecticut retreat house:
an estate with gardeners, servants
the same color as us and the other poets
who now share the space. I'd have read Keats,

or Browning out loud, balancing
gravitas and romantic flourishes.
We'd be courting, not married,
for what know the married—
so it's said—of moments that stir our eros?

Why should we imagine ourselves
more than betrothed *and* attracted
to each other, still stirred by the feeling
of palm on nape of neck? Dare we
circle this pond without argument
over chores and money? Dare we

let our eyes linger on lips, the smooth skin
between neck and collarbone

as we speak of metaphor, recite modern
poems with or without ulterior motive?
Dare we believe this time well spent?

Knot

If you believe the myths of statistics,
I'll leave when my wife's belly swells,

terrified of diapers, irked by crying,
drawn to shadow, siren songs,

urban streets. If you hear wisdom
in multiplex movie fathers, Nielsen dads,

sports-radio hosts, I can't bother with nurturing
or sensitivity— I will want a boy, will bark

"Suck it up!" when he falls, will try to trade
Barbies for boxing gloves if saddled with a girl.

But popular thought and culture give you
no name for the ache and envy engendered

in me by the sight of a newborn, no name
for the awakening of my grad-school baby lust.

If I subscribe to history's lessons, I should
blame my wife for this wait, imagine something

disfigured in her, but I nearly severed ties
with my mother when her careless pronoun

placed the burden of infertility on my wife.
The only history I can reference is brothers

who waited years for progeny, but one myth
that's part truth is men don't always share sadness

that rests on foundations of vulnerability.
Besides "take cold showers" I've learned little

from them, but what, really, could they tell me
that might unravel this Gordian frustration,

this monthly and monthly mystery?

Dual Income, No Kids

Bring me clumsy with worry,
awkwardly cradling head, arms.
Bring me filthy with exhaustion,
bring me chaos of diapers, toys,
little socks everywhere and nowhere,
books underfoot, the dog colored
with crayon— test my patience
for clutter, prolonged untidiness.
Bring me papers to grade in snatches
of time, meals claimed between bottles
and baths, stupefying tears, unchecked
by cuddling, feeding, driving, singing.
Bring me sad to leave daycare,
bring me rushing from the office
for fevers, infections bring me
tantrums, negotiations—

Bring us compromised intimacy,
movies at home, thrifty vacations,
more chicken, less steak.
Bring us meals out for time,
not romance, bring us impatient
with each other over nighttime diapers,
discipline methods. Bring us squeezing
the budget for piano, ballet,
bring us weekends scheduled
as tightly as weeks. Bring us
knowledge of trials left out
of this poem, hope unsuppressed
by months upon months
upon months of empty.

Early Rising

Your daughter does not drive the car that cuts you off.
She is not collecting garbage for the truck
    in front of you on the one-lane street
    when you are late for work.
She is not the operator whose unsteady grasp
    of your native tongue makes you repeat
    your problem three times.
She is not the sold-out movie, though she sits
    at home with the babysitter.
She is not the lines at the grocery store
    after the forecast for snow.
She is not the student who in May still cannot
    finish a sentence without saying "like."
She is not the inconsistent wireless signal in your house.
She is not the computer when it boots too slow.
She is not your father, who must have bequeathed you
    his impatience, like some curse of a birthright.

Legacy

The same man who nearly cried at the lilting flute notes
of Hubert Laws' "Theme from Love Story,"

then said, "Don't ever let anyone tell you black men can't
be sensitive" stomped on the brake pedal, threw

the '94 Ford Aerostar into park and shoved open
the driver's side door. That he was stopping

in the middle of a narrow street to accost the driver
in the car ahead of us was not—for the butler

turned soldier turned artist turned editor—as important
as his pride. My silent embarrassment filled the car,

drowning out the Center City Philly noise
that had flooded through the door he left open.

The shame lingered longer than the desire for control
or right of way that compelled my father from his seat.

But that same desire spikes my heart rate when my two-year-old yells
"No! I do it!" if we're late and I want her seatbelt clicked quickly.

When her wailing floods the supermarket, invites sidelong
stink-eyes I understand my father's high blood pressure even

as I give into mine when we get back to the car. I don't usually
frown in the mirror, but I recognize the glower

that sometimes darkens her face. I wonder what balance
sounds like, how long calm lasts, if a flute can drown out a car horn.

day, 9:30am

After their hands are washed
After their utensils are chosen
After little brother needs help
After "Get back to the table!"
After "I have to go bathroom!"
After dropped spoons, spun forks, licked knives
After crumpled but spotless napkins
After spilled milk, spilled apple juice
After "that's enough syrup"
After the potato-fed dog,
After the pancake-fed dog,
After the sausage-fed dog,
After my wife tells me I have to get used to this.
Before half-naked running toddlers,
Before "But that's what *I* want to wear"
Before jumping off the couch,
Before jumping on the couch
Before "Do you want to go to the park or not?"
Before the snacks are packed
Before the slathering of toothpaste
Before the gummy vitamins
Before shoe battles
Before "Get. In. The. Car."
There is the lull:
dining room table cleared,
dishwasher humming, drain gurgling
I nurse the last quarter-mug of coffee,
Gird myself, ascend to the beautiful chaos.

Empathy

Zoë says she will get me a new daddy
days after we hear our dog's prostate
has swelled asymmetrically. In the vet's
placid, gentle baritone I heard my brother

Brian, who years ago quavered as he tried
to balance experienced nurse calm
with the sudden erosion of telling his
younger siblings our father had cancer.

Id starts to stay in his crate, skip
dinner and again breakfast, lopes
to the patch to strain again. He resists
stairs, avoids running. I can't decide

if I am happy that Zoë will be trained early
in the ways of grief, or flummoxed
by the task of helping her little brother
understand the dog's eventual disappearance.

At least we have this preparation. Spared
the suddenness of screeching tires, gore,
an apologetic motorist, we find uneasy
comfort in the weeks-long farewell.

Presence

Dirt on the boots we wore to dig the hole.
Hairs collected in the vacuum a month ago.
Pet store receipt for diapers.
Unstolen food on the dining room table.
Unclaimed food under the dining room table.
Loose hair in broom bristles.
The quiet delivery of mail.
Oatmeal shampoo on the shelf in the laundry room.
Lamb and chicken blend in the pantry.
The chewed up tennis ball under the couch.
The chewed up tennis ball behind the bookcase.
The chewed up tennis ball in the coat closet.
The chewed up tennis ball in the toy box.
Hairballs in places we haven't dusted yet.
Sympathy card from the vet's office.
Walking downstairs alone at 5:30am.

How To Test a Marriage

Start by taking away their sleep. Leave them bleary,
fatigued, desperately ticking off the list
of what will quiet the baby.
When diapers work, or feeding, or just a move
to a different room let them fall back asleep
smiling, proud of themselves, each other
bound even closer by this new struggle.

Now undermine that confidence
with disparate opinions on sleep training.
Give her tears to shut down the conversation,
create festering resentment. Tell them to discipline
in two voices only occasionally united and let
the child play one against the other. Tell her he
is too stern, tell him she isn't tough enough
and watch them overcompensate.

Make certain his notions of parenting
were mostly romanticized—for every walk
in the park tell the child not to listen—
watch him draw lines in the sand.
Watch the two year-old dance across them.

Let the second sneak into her womb
behind infertility's lingering shadow turned hubris.
Fill their snatches of time spent together with pure planning:
Who gets the car, what's for dinner, who is on the Metro,
will the kids be warm enough? Tell her he doesn't know
how much clothing is enough. Tell him
her idea of cold is overprotective.

Make sure she babysat a lot. Make her sister
ten years younger, make her think he never had either
so she knows implicitly more. Make that true
but tell her to tote it out more than he wants to hear.

Make sure his parents split when he was three.
Make sure her parents split when her memories
of it were far more vivid—give them eight years without kids
and the determination to stay together.
See if they can make it work.

Make it Work for You

When I ask my daughter if she wants tacos
I get to eat one of my favorite dishes.
When I buy organic fruit strips for Zoë
and her infant brother, I get half of his.

We parents talk freely about bed times,
potty training, daycare situations, schools—
but I've never heard "Hey, I hustled my daughter
to read the book *I* wanted last night."

The promise of ice cream after lunch
unfurrows the asparagus-affected brow,
guarantees the dulce de leche you've craved.
Raise your voice half an octave and bathtime
sounds exciting, brings bedtime closer.

A trip to Target after they are both asleep
is alone time—I blast the radio, or call
my mother, my west-coast brother.
Often I'm happy for the silence, so I
take it, each time, with less guilt. I take it.

Life of Riley

I'm playing this language thing
for all it's worth. They brought
someone here to ask me questions,
check a bunch of boxes and scribble.
She never came back so I figure

I'm in the clear, can keep
saying as much as I need
to get what I want. The big one,
my "sister" I think they call her,
doesn't realize she's giving me
free lessons: what makes them smile
and what raises their voices.

Daddy makes funny faces
when he steps on my toys.
Every now and then I throw
an old word, *nurse*—at Mommy—
figure she might forget
one day, cradle me again.

The dog? Don't get me started
on how funny he is when I know
he'd bite me if he didn't appreciate
how easy he's got it. So I keep
pulling his tail, yanking his ear.

Don't know how much longer
I can stand repeating myself, though—
might have to defy some expectations,
clarify a consonant or two.
But...eh, really— why give it up?

And Wouldn't You?

Deny me the presence of my nearest
for 12 hours, then bring her through the door
just as sleep has settled its gaze but not massage on me
and I will rally, jump, run to her
refuse the darkness of my bedroom
for another glass of water
for one more wobble to the bathroom
one more fallen stuffed animal
one more two-day old boo-boo inspection
one more side dish I must mention from lunch
one more recollected slight from recess
one more question about beetles
one more what I want for breakfast
one more what I want for Christmas
                        my next birthday
                        my birthday after that.
Water.
Bathroom.

So when Mommy returns
ninety minutes past bedtime
why *shouldn't* he fight
until she lays next to him?
Let him nuzzle her soft parts,
Let him remember what he knows of her
by feeling more than by name, his mind
whispering breastmilk memories.
Only when he settles first arm,
then leg across her chest, around
her thigh will his fidgeting slow,
his head loll, his lips part
his breathing find a quiet rhythm.

Baby Gate

He hated the metal—cold, even when the house
was warm. He disliked the restriction of movement,

the forced request for upstairs or down. Maybe
the dexterity required to unlock it reminded him

he is small enough to be picked up, willed:
"brush teeth, put on a coat, time to go."

Perhaps it was simply the closest outlet
for his infant-become-toddler boy energy.

He achieved its dislodging in one final crescendo
of tantrum, archway wood denting with each

scream-punctuated slam. The metaphor of our now
failed attempt to contain steadily growing small people

probably lost on him, I nonetheless held
on to the notion we still need to protect them

from the steps. I created uneasy reassurance
by tinkering—patching, for now, their safety.

New School

Age appropriate, his stutter
mild violence, selective hearing
not unusual symptoms of transition.

But his four resembles yours,
reminds you of the big eyes
that swallowed the sound of parents

roaring at each other, full throats
teaching you the decibel level
employed now in futility when his spirit

reflects yours and your volume
becomes your parents'. This is all
you know of discipline—who remembers,

years later, their parent's deft redirect?
How can you unlearn your need for control
when a nurse looked into your three-day-old eyes,

said "This one will want things just so."
This is, after all, generational—Oma
fussed, never cajoled, "Where's your napkin!?"

And from her, or Nana, who raised
above your father's misbehaving head
the specter of his mother's never return,

he learned lines in the sand, learned
ultimatums, learned whatever made you ask
your older brother "Why does dad get so angry?"

So when your son's stutter betrays the tension
of missing friends, navigating new spaces,
when your wife's long patience vanishes

behind a recycling bin hurled from small hands,
you intercede, sweep him into a hug. You can't
rescue yourself from the top of the stairs,

but you can ask if Gus misses his preschool
yes and what he misses *Eric* and who else
Sammy and you can promise play dates, make

the calls as soon as he's asleep, grinding his teeth,
tossing, kicking like you used to. You can do this
for him, you tell yourself, for him.

Notes

"Nigger Apple"
> "Just like it says in the encyclopedia!" refers to a line from Dave Chappelle's *Killing Them Softly* in which he imagines a white person reacting to the site of a black person eating fried chicken.

"Inundated": *After watching Hurricane Katrina coverage on CNN*

"Ali, Bomaye"
> The poem's title is a phrase chanted by residents of Zaire in the days leading up to, during, and after the 1974 heavyweight title fight between Muhammed Ali and George Foreman. In Lingala it means, "Ali, kill him." The people of Zaire admired Ali, especially for his refusal to fight in Vietnam, and were uneasy with Foreman, in part because he brought with him to Zaire his pet German Shepherd, the same breed of dog used by the Dutch during their colonization of Zaire, now known as the Democratic Republic of the Congo.

"Ivory": *After a photograph of Kenyan elephant poachers*

The speaker in the poems in section III is Jim, the runaway slave from Mark Twain's *Adventures of Huckleberry Finn*

"Angels"
> Epigraph: *"It's a dead man. Yes, indeedy; naked, too. He's ben shot in de back. I reck'n he's ben dead two er three days. Come in, Huck, but doan' look at his face -- it's too gashly."*

"Jim on the Raft after His "Dream""
> Cairo, Illinois, was a city from which Huck and Jim believed Jim could access the Illinois territory, a free state in the time that the book takes place.
> *"Dat truck dah is* trash*; en trash is what people is dat puts dirt on de head er dey fren's en makes 'em ashamed."* Jim, AHF Chapter 15

"The 'King and Duke' Join the Raft"

> Petersburg, Missouri, Huck's home town, modeled after Hannibal, MO, Mark Twain's home town.
>
> *"...the duke said he had ciphered out his idea about how to run in daylight without it being dangersome for Jim; so he allowed he would go down to the town and fix that thing. The king allowed he would go, too, and see if he couldn't strike something. We was out of coffee, so Jim said I better go along with them in the canoe and get some."* Huck, AHF Ch. 20

"Sent Her Sprawling"

> *"He was thinking about his wife and his children, away up yonder, and he was low and homesick"* Huck, AHF, Ch. 23

"Bound"

> *"Jim he spoke to the duke, and said he hoped it wouldn't take but a few hours, because it got mighty heavy and tiresome to him when he had to lay all day in the wigwam tied with the rope."* Huck, AHF Ch. 24
>
> Wigwam: small hut-like structure on a raft

"The 'Rescue'"

> *"Tom most lost all patience with him; and said he was just loadened down with more gaudier chances than a prisoner ever had in the world to make a name for himself, and yet he didn't know enough to appreciate them, and they was just about wasted on him."* Huck, AHF, Ch. 38

"Groove": *For Cornelius and Sarah*

"Library": *for Paul Levy*

"Dual Income, No Kids"

> Epigraph: *"I love you more than sleep"* ‑from my wedding vows.

"Presence": *For Dan and his dog Roofus.*

Hayes Davis holds a Masters of Fine Arts from the University of Maryland, where he won an Academy of American Poets Prize; he is a member of Cave Canem's first cohort of fellows, a former Bread Loaf working scholar, and a former Geraldine Miles Poet-Scholar at the Squaw Valley Community of Writers.

He has also attended writing retreats at Manhattanville College and Soul Mountain. His work has appeared in a range of literary journals and anthologies. He teaches English at a private school in Washington, D.C. and lives in Silver Spring with his wife, poet Teri Ellen Cross Davis, and their children.

Let Our Eyes Linger is his first book of poems.

Gratitude

Writing these poems and publishing this book would not have been possible without support, guidance, and/or opportunities from the following people:

My parents, Beth D. Bader and Earl E. Davis, Jr., who offered and continue to offer encouragement and unconditional support.
My wife, Teri Ellen Cross Davis; my first reader and editor, my partner in crime and parenting.
Reginald Dwayne Betts, Kyle Dargan, Toi Derricotte, Honoree Fanone Jeffers, Stanley Plumly, and Joshua Weiner, who brought helpful editorial eyes and supportive words to this manuscript.
I also owe gratitude to: my teachers, especially Elizabeth Alexander, Lucille Clifton, Michael Collier, Cornelius Eady, Carol Lefelt, Phillis Levin, Marilyn Nelson, Jeff Oaks, Carl Philips, Patricia Smith, Sonia Sanchez, and David Walton; to the Cave Canem Family, especially Holly Bass, Herman Beavers, Derrick Weston Brown, Omari Daniel, Joel Dias-Porter, T'ai Freedom Ford, Reginald Harris, Tonya Hegamin, Linda Susan Jackson, Brandon D. Johnson, Nzadi Keita, Alan King, Toni Asante Lightfoot, Ernesto Mercer, Camille Rankine, Katy Richey, and Venus Thrash; workshop peers Sandra Beasley, Paulette Beete, Sarah Browning, Yael Flusberg, Yao Glover, Melanie Henderson, Fred Joiner, and Joseph Ross; the Bread Loaf Writers' Conference, the Creative Writing MFA Program at the University of Maryland, especially Don Berger; the Manhattanville Summer Writers' Retreat, and the Squaw Valley Community of Writers; teaching colleagues John Burghardt, Louise Brennan, Dan Entwisle, Jay Frazier, Eduardo Gonzalez, Thu Anh Nguyen, Ashish Patwardhan, Jennifer Solomon, and Christopher Thompson. I am also grateful to Michael Gushue, Dan Vera, and Poetry Mutual Press.

Colophon

This poetry in this book has been laid out using two beautiful types: Centaur for text and Nicholas for titling. Both of these types are modern revivals of the work of the fifteenth-century printer Nicolas Jenson. Jenson introduced the invention of printing to Italy and his Venetian types are regarded as among the very best of the Renaissance, indeed of all time.

Centaur is a refinement of Roman inscriptional capitals designed by Bruce Rogers as a titling design for signage in the Metropolitan Museum of Art in New York City. Rogers later designed a lowercase based on Jenson's work, turning the titling into a full typeface, Centaur, the most elegant and Aldine of the Jenson derivatives. Nicholas was designed by the Toronto-based type designer Nick Shinn as a headline version of his Jenson type Goodchild.

Poetry Mutual Press is committed to presenting the very best of modern poetry. We are committed to creating beautiful pieces of visual/verbal art that you can enjoy and treasure.

We are proud to present Hayes Davis' *Let Our Eyes Linger* as a work that continues our growth as a home for vibrant modern poetry.

For more of our titles and to find out more about us, visit us at

www.POETRYMUTUAL.org

Or write us at: POETRY MUTUAL PRESS
3323 14th St. NE
Washington, DC 20017

press@poetrymutual.org

Made in the USA
Middletown, DE
22 January 2023

22865586R00052